The Pros and Cons of Geothermal Power

Angela Britcher

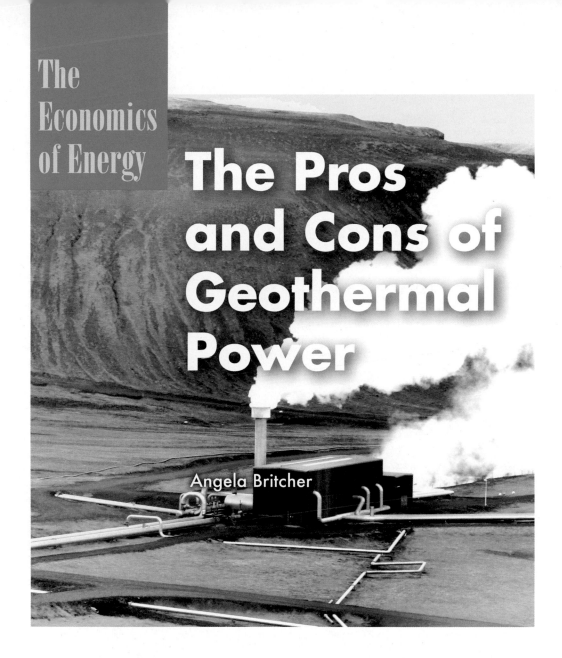

Cavendish
Square

New York

Published in 2016 by Cavendish Square Publishing, LLC
243 5th Avenue, Suite 136, New York, NY 10016

Copyright © 2016 by Cavendish Square Publishing, LLC

First Edition

Website: cavendishsq.com

This publication represents the opinions and views of the author based on his or her personal experience, knowledge, and research. The information in this book serves as a general guide only. The author and publisher have used their best efforts in preparing this book and disclaim liability rising directly or indirectly from the use and application of this book.

CPSIA Compliance Information: Batch #CW16CSQ

All websites were available and accurate when this book was sent to press.

Cataloging-in-Publication Data

Britcher, Angela.
The pros and cons of geothermal power / by Angela Britcher.
p. cm. — (The economics of energy)
Includes index.
ISBN 978-1-5026-0956-4 (hardcover) 978-1-5026-0957-1 (ebook)
1. Geothermal engineering — Juvenile literature. 2. Geothermal resources — Juvenile literature. I. Britcher, Angela. II. Title.
TK1055.B75 2016
333.8'8—d23

Editorial Director: David McNamara
Editor: Amy Hayes/Ryan Nagelhout
Copy Editor: Nathan Heidelberger
Art Director: Jeffrey Talbot

Designer: Amy Greenan
Production Manager: Jennifer Ryder-Talbot
Production Editor: Renni Johnson
Photo Researcher: J8 Media

Printed in the United States of America

The Economics of Energy

Table of Contents

5 Chapter 1
Harnessing the Earth's Heat

23 Chapter 2
The Advantages of Geothermal Energy

39 Chapter 3
The Disadvantages of Geothermal Energy

55 Chapter 4
The Future of Geothermal Energy

73 Glossary

75 Find Out More

78 Index

80 About the Author

The Tungurahua volcano in the Andes Mountains of Ecuador has erupted regularly since 1999. Volcanoes are one example of a place on Earth's crust where geothermal energy reaches the surface.

Chapter 1

Harnessing the Earth's Heat

There is hot stuff brewing underground.

Think about the heat and lava that bursts from volcanoes. Have you ever seen Yellowstone National Park's geyser Old Faithful shooting boiling water 140 feet (43 meters) into the air? It takes a lot of energy and heat to shoot this boiling water high into the air. This kind of heat and energy is called **geothermal energy**. When it is harnessed from inside the Earth it can be used to heat buildings and homes.

Geothermal energy has been used since ancient times to heat water and homes, but it is just in the last hundred years that it is being used commercially to replace gas, oil, and coal to generate electricity to power buildings, universities, and even entire cities.

Geothermal energy is considered a clean, environmentally friendly, and reliable energy source. Since **Earth's core** is constantly generating heat, geothermal energy is considered a **renewable** source of energy. As people around the world try to reduce reliance on **fossil fuels**, geothermal energy offers an alternative. However, it is not widely used. The costs to install a geothermal system have been significantly higher

Old Faithful, a geyser in Yellowstone National Park, sprays water and steam more than 90 feet (27 meters) in the air almost every 90 minutes.

than other heating and cooling systems, but that is changing. Once a system is installed, it takes less energy to run, meaning an increase in savings over time. Certain geographic locations are better than others for geothermal projects, and it is a challenge to transport geothermal energy too far from its source. Scientists and energy experts are working to make this renewable, safe energy source more readily available.

The Earth's Natural Heat

"Geo" means Earth and "thermal" means heat. Together, "geothermal" means Earth's heat. It's a natural process. Even temperatures just a few feet below the ground steadily remain between 50 and 60 degrees

Fahrenheit (10 and 15.5 degrees Celsius). In most places around the world, the deeper into the Earth you go, the hotter it is.

To find where geothermal energy is created you have to go into Earth's core. Earth is made of several layers formed billions of years ago. The outermost layer is the crust. It is made up of mostly rocks that form two kinds of plates: the continental plates, which are above sea level, form the continents, and oceanic plates make up the ocean floor.

Beneath the crust are the upper mantle and lower mantle. Here is where Earth starts heating up. This layer is 1,800 miles (2,900 kilometers) thick and is made up of rocks and liquid magma. When it shoots out of an erupting volcano, magma becomes lava.

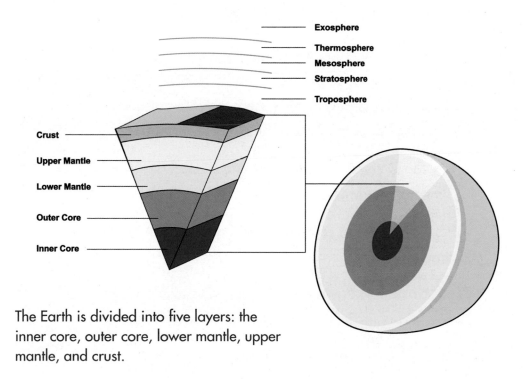

The Earth is divided into five layers: the inner core, outer core, lower mantle, upper mantle, and crust.

A Timeline of Geothermal Energy Use

33 BCE Public and private baths in Rome use geothermal energy and hot springs to heat water for therapy

1820s Scientist Francesco Larderel discovers that he can use hot springs to create steam-powered energy instead of burning wood

1830 Hot Springs, Arkansas, is fully settled

1847 The Geysers geothermal field in California is first seen by European-American settlers John Frémont and William Bell Elliott; the field had been used by Native Americans for therapeutic baths for thousands of years

1848 The Geysers is developed into a hotel and spa known for its healing waters

1892 Boise, Idaho, creates the first geothermal district heating system

1904 Larderello Power Plant in Italy completes the first successful public demonstration of geothermal energy, using it to power a light bulb

1960s The Geysers is converted into a dry-steam power plant using geothermal energy

1970 The Geothermal Resources Council forms. Its purpose is to encourage worldwide development of geothermal resources. The Geothermal Steam Act is enacted; it gives the secretary of the interior the authority to lease public and some federal lands for geothermal exploration and development

1977 The United States Department of Energy is formed

2005 The Energy Policy Act is signed into law; this makes it less expensive and more appealing for homeowners and businesses to switch to geothermal energy systems.

Pieces of Earth's crust move over the upper mantle in what is called plate tectonics. When the plates collide, earthquakes and volcanic eruptions may occur. In the upper mantle, temperatures are around 1,600°F (871°C). As you move deeper into the lower mantle, closer to the Earth's core, temperatures rise to 4,000°F (2,200°C).

The outer core is below the mantle. It is made up of metals that are so hot they remain in a liquid state. It is 1,400 miles (2,250 km) thick and temperatures range from 4,000°F to 9,000°F (2,200°C to 5,000°C). The inner core is the center of the Earth. Scientists have never seen the inner core, but they theorize that it is a solid ball made mostly of iron and that it is at least 9,000°F (5,000°C). When the planet was formed billions of years ago, the heaviest metals moved to the center, while lighter materials such as air and water stayed on the surface. The pressure of Earth's gravity on the inner core is so great that the iron ball cannot melt. Because of the metals in the core, the whole Earth is magnetized. This is what makes the North and South Poles.

Earth's layers are constantly moving and changing. When magma from below the crust rises, it heats water close to Earth's surface, including rainwater that has seeped down through the ground over thousands of years. When the water gets hot, it turns to steam. Steam is lighter than water, so it moves up toward the surface. That steam can be harnessed to create electricity, power turbines, and heat and cool buildings.

Sometimes the water becomes trapped in porous rocks, creating what are called "geothermal reservoirs." Scientists drill into the rocks to find these reservoirs and use the geothermal energy. To harness more energy than what naturally flows to the surface, wells are dug about 1 mile (1.6 km) deep. Pipes bring very hot water to power turbines on the surface.

In the United States, this is mostly to create power in western states like California and Washington. Throughout the rest of the country, geothermal energy can be used to heat and cool homes. Specialists dig a hole in the yard near the home, insert pipes into the ground, and then fill them with water or a mix of water and antifreeze. In the winter, the belowground pipes are warmer than the air above. A pump pulls the warm water from below and extracts heat from it, warming the house. In the summer, the ground is cooler than the air, so pumps pull cool air into the home and circulate it.

Where Is Geothermal Energy Found?

The obvious places where we can see geothermal energy reservoirs are where there are volcanoes, hot springs, and geysers. These geographic hot spots are prime locations to efficiently collect Earth's heat. However, it is a challenge to transport geothermal energy far from its source. Steam and boiling water need to be used to create energy quickly. Building power plants in locations near reservoirs is important.

The Ring of Fire

The most concentrated area of volcanoes in the world is called the Ring of Fire. It is an area around the Pacific Ocean dotted with volcanoes where more than 90 percent of all earthquakes occur and 75 percent of volcanic activity happens. It includes volcanoes such as Mount Saint Helens in Washington, Mount Fuji in Japan, and Krakatoa in Indonesia. The Ring of Fire is also known for the faults such as the San Andreas Fault in California. These faults are where tectonic plates slide past or otherwise

A DEEPER DIVE

Iceland

Iceland is not in the Ring of Fire but it is a pioneer in producing and using geothermal energy. In the last hundred years, Iceland switched from primarily burning peat and coal for energy to renewable sources such as geothermal. According to the country's National Energy Authority, nine out of ten households use volcanic-heated water for home heating. Icelandic people also use geothermal heat for producing energy, melting snow, heating greenhouses, farming fish, and heating their swimming pools.

Iceland is located where two tectonic plates come together to form the Mid-Atlantic Ridge. The plates are constantly moving apart, releasing volcanic heat, energy, and lava. Iceland is home to more than two hundred volcanoes!

It is important to Iceland to use geothermal energy in a sustainable manner. While it is renewable, no one is sure of the consequences of using it excessively. The country has guidelines for drilling and use for energy companies. Iceland is also conducting a long-term study on the best ways to capture and use geothermal energy by digging deeper wells.

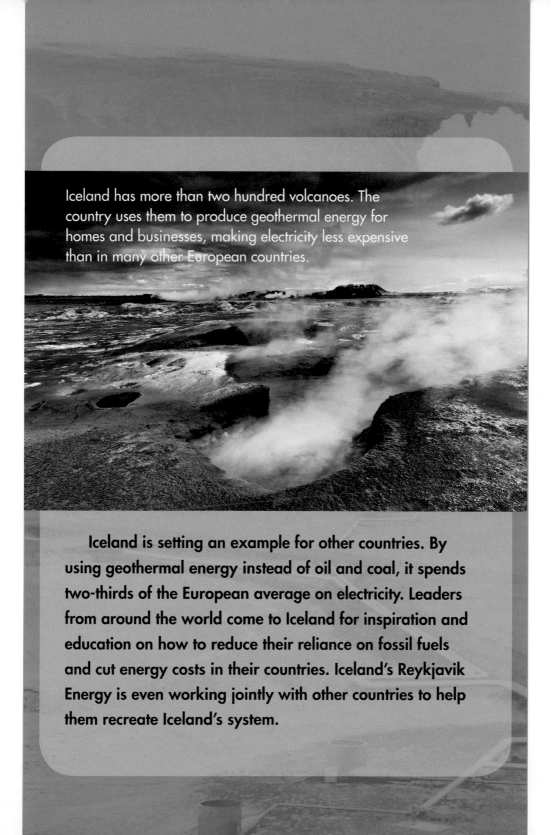

Iceland has more than two hundred volcanoes. The country uses them to produce geothermal energy for homes and businesses, making electricity less expensive than in many other European countries.

Iceland is setting an example for other countries. By using geothermal energy instead of oil and coal, it spends two-thirds of the European average on electricity. Leaders from around the world come to Iceland for inspiration and education on how to reduce their reliance on fossil fuels and cut energy costs in their countries. Iceland's Reykjavik Energy is even working jointly with other countries to help them recreate Iceland's system.

The Ring of Fire is a large area of volcanoes circling the Pacific Ocean. More earthquakes and volcanic eruptions happen in the Ring of Fire than anywhere in the world. It is a hot spot for geothermal energy production.

move up against one another. Sometimes this results in earthquakes and volcanic eruptions, creating geothermal energy. Countries along the Ring of Fire generate most of the world's geothermal power.

The United States creates more than 16 million megawatts of geothermal-based power. That is more than anywhere in the world! But while the United States is producing more geothermal energy, it still uses more fossil fuels than geothermal energy resources. In other countries,

The green areas of the map highlight countries producing geothermal energy. The United States creates more geothermal energy than other countries but continues to rely on fossil fuels for much of its energy consumption.

geothermal power is getting more use. The Philippines, Indonesia, Mexico, New Zealand, Italy, and Iceland are all large producers and consumers of geothermal energy.

How Does the Earth's Heat Make Energy?

Now that you know where geothermal energy comes from, it's time to see how we can harness it to create energy in buildings and our homes. There are three main ways to use geothermal energy: direct use and district heating systems, generating electricity in a power plant, and geothermal heat pumps.

Direct Use and District Heating Systems

This is the oldest use of geothermal energy. For centuries, cultures such as the Romans and Native Americans used hot springs to cook, heat, and bathe. They believed bathing in mineral-rich hot springs was healing. In direct heating, hot water is piped into buildings. In ancient Rome, wells were drilled and the water was directed into pipes to guide water into large baths and early faucets. It is not very similar today. Steam and water are directed by a system of pipes, sometimes mixed with another liquid, into a home or building. It goes through a compressor, which builds hot water pressure. Then the water travels through a heat exchanger, where the heat is transferred from the water to the building's heating system. The water is then recycled by being absorbed back into the ground. A district heating system is a more complex system where more buildings such as a university campus or city blocks are fed by a geothermal reservoir.

Geothermal Power Plants

Geothermal power plants are located in areas rich in geothermal reservoirs such as California, Iceland, and Italy. Wells are dug 1 to 2 miles (1.6 to 3.2 km) deep and hot water is pumped from nearby geothermal reservoirs into the power plants. There are a few ways the power plants work: dry steam, flash steam, and binary transfer. Very hot steam, between 300°F and 700°F (150°C and 370°C), turns turbines in a dry steam plant. Flash steam plants use hot water at high pressures converted to steam to power turbines. With flash steam plants, the water is reused and recycled. Once it cools from steam back into a liquid, it is reabsorbed into the ground and can be reused. The third way geothermal power plants work is called binary. They transfer the heat from hot water pulled up from the Earth into another liquid. The heat causes the second liquid to turn into steam that powers turbines.

Heat Pumps

Geothermal heat pumps are the most common type of geothermal energy source used in homes. They move heat that is underground but near the Earth's surface to control building temperatures above ground. There are two basic systems: air-source and ground-source. They work by pumping warmer air and water or cooler air and water from the ground or surrounding air into a building. It can work to both heat and cool, depending on the season. In the winter, if you dig a foot or more below the ground, the belowground temperature is usually warmer than the outside, aboveground temperature. In many areas that use geothermal energy, the ground remains between 50°F and 60°F (10°C and 15.5°C). Water from the warmer ground is pumped into a home's heating system. In the summer, it works in the same way, but the temperatures are reversed. The ground water is cooler than the outside air.

A Brief History of Geothermal Development

For centuries, people around the world have used hot springs. Romans piped the warm water into homes and buildings with large baths for the first bathtubs. Native Americans introduced early US settlers to "taking the waters." The minerals in hot springs throughout the colonies were said to cure all kinds of ailments. They also served a social function: geothermal energy was originally used for spas! In 1830, Hot Springs, Arkansas, was settled. A businessman named Asa Thompson started selling bath time in the springs in a big tub for $1. Since then, the warmth from within Earth that heats the springs has been channeled to heat power plants, buildings, and homes.

A DEEPER DIVE

Larderello

In 1904, the Larderello power plant in Italy gave the world its first documented demonstration of using geothermal energy for industrial use. The plant used a small generator powered by steam from the ground to light five light bulbs. The area was originally called the Valle de Diavolo, or "Devil's Valley," because of the boiling water, steam, and smell of sulfur that rose from the ground there.

The power plant is in the Cecina Valley in Tuscany. It is an area known for its beautiful rolling hills that happen to have puffs of steam escaping through the ground. The museum on the site is a tourist stop where visitors can see the origins of geothermal power in the region, archeological evidence of how Romans and Etruscans used the steam and heat, and multimedia demonstrations of how modern geothermal energy produces more than 5 billion kilowatt-hours of renewable power each year.

Larderello, Italy, is home to the first commercial geothermal power plant. The area in Tuscany was originally called the "Valle de Diavolo" or "Devil's Valley" because of the steam rising from the ground and the smell of sulfur.

Geothermal energy got its start as an alternative to fuels such as lumber and coal in Italy in the 1820s. Scientist Francesco Larderel was trying to save trees and the forests. He discovered he could use hot springs to create steam-powered energy instead of burning wood. This became the first geothermal power plant in 1904, named **Larderello**.

Larderello is an area with active volcanic activity but no eruptions since the eleventh century. It is considered a dry steam field and produces 10 percent of the world's geothermal power while providing electricity to a million Italian households. However, there are some questions about Larderello's sustainability. There has been a 30 percent drop in steam pressure there since the 1950s.

About the same time as Larderel was using geothermal energy to power buildings, William Bell Elliott found a steaming valley in California near what became San Francisco, which he called **The Geysers**. There he built a famous hotel, The Geysers Resort Hotel, with a natural springs spa where famous figures such as Mark Twain, J. P. Morgan, and Theodore Roosevelt vacationed. Eventually, in 1960, The Geysers Resort Hotel became a power plant. It was the first large-scale geothermal plant to create electricity from turbines.

Meanwhile, other geothermal development had taken place across the country for decades. For example, in 1892 in Boise, Idaho, geothermal energy was first used as a heating system. Water was piped from hot springs to homes and businesses in a district heating system. Today there are four systems in Boise that provide heat to 5 million square feet (464,515 square meters) of buildings.

By the 1970s, geothermal energy was becoming more understood and utilized. This created a need for organizations to work toward developing more resources for using geothermal energy. The Geothermal Resources Council was formed during this time. Its intention was to encourage developing geothermal resources worldwide.

Also in 1970, the Geothermal Steam Act was enacted. This granted the US secretary of the interior the ability to lease public and some federal lands for geothermal development. The Geothermal Energy Association was formed and became a lobbying group for US companies that develop geothermal resources worldwide for electrical power generation and direct-heat uses. The National Science Foundation became the lead agency for federal geothermal programs. In 1977, the Department of Energy was formed, overseeing how all kinds of energy were being produced and used in the United States. In 1994, the Department of Energy started working on ways to reduce **greenhouse gas** emissions. It teamed up with energy companies and government organizations to find ways to develop more geothermal resources to create electricity and heat pumps.

In the twenty-first century, the Energy Policy Act of 2005 was signed into law. This made it less expensive and more appealing for homeowners and businesses to switch to geothermal energy systems.

CRITICAL THINKING

- Why is geothermal energy considered renewable? What is a renewable resource?

- How has geothermal use changed? How has it stayed the same?

- Why is it important to build geothermal power plants close to volcanic areas?

The Nesjavellir Geothermal Power Station is the second largest geothermal power station in Iceland. The power station produces enough heat and hot water to serve the people of Iceland's capital city, Reykjavik.

Chapter 2

The Advantages of Geothermal Energy

Geothermal energy use is on the rise around the world. In this chapter, you learn about the advantages of using geothermal power and why energy companies, heating and air conditioning companies, and governments are investing more resources into building geothermal power plants and geothermal home systems. Here you will also learn about how geothermal energy is a renewable energy source and why it is important and beneficial to replace fossil fuels. You will also learn how geothermal energy sources emit less pollution and greenhouse gases while being available no matter the weather.

Renewable Energy Source

There are many sources of renewable energy, including **wind energy**, **solar energy**, and water energy (often called hydro energy). Geothermal energy is also a renewable energy source. This means that the Earth naturally makes more all the time. Geothermal energy is always available, churning underground. As you learned in Chapter 1, magma, or molten rock, from

Earth's core heats the crust above it. Heat is constantly radiating from Earth's core, rising through its layers.

Fossil Fuels

Fossil fuels include oil, natural gas, and coal. Fossil fuels are not considered renewable because it takes Earth thousands of years to make them. There are many efforts to reduce how much of these nonrenewable fuel sources we use. How do we use fossil fuels? They power our cars, heat our homes, and are used to create products we use every day such as plastics and the rubber in sneakers, basketballs, and soccer balls.

Let's look at fossil fuels to learn why geothermal energy is considered a more reliable and clean source of energy compared to them.

Coal is made from decomposing plants such as trees and ferns that typically died near water. Over time the plants were buried below the ground, usually in swampy areas. Enormous pressure pushed on the plants over millions of years and turned them to coal.

There are pros and cons to coal. When coal is burned, sulfur is released which can pollute the air. Coal contributes to breathing issues and lung diseases. Miners are exposed to sulfur dioxide, which is harmful to our lungs, and they face the risk of mines collapsing and trapping them inside.

So, why have people used coal for so long? It is inexpensive and abundant in the United States. Power plants and mines are developing safer ways to mine and burn coal so that fewer toxins are released. The coal industry also keeps Americans working, employing hundreds of thousands of people across the country.

Coal is mined at a plant in West Virginia. The mining and burning of coal releases much more pollution into the environment than the collection and use of geothermal power.

Oil and natural gas are made in much the same way as coal. Instead of plants, organic animal materials and animals such as zooplankton died and were buried in the ground below the oceans. Just like coal, heat and pressure act on the decomposing animals, changing the matter into oil and gas. First, thick oil is formed. If the material is under more pressure and heat, then natural gas is created.

One of the biggest problems with fossil fuels is it takes so long to create more of them. It takes millions of years to create fuel from dead

A DEEPER DIVE

What Is a Fossil?

We hear a lot in the news about how bad the emissions from fossil fuels are for the environment or how we need to use less of them. While those criticisms are true, fossil fuels are created over thousands of years from plants and animals. They are natural. **Fossils** are the root of what creates fossil fuels.

A fossil is a trace or the actual remains of an animal or plant. You might see an imprint of a fern or an animal on a rock. However, fossils are not just imprints on rocks. Scientists also find actual pieces of animals that are considered fossils. Most of these are invertebrates such as crabs, insects, snails, starfish, worms, and other animals that do not have hard spines. When those animals die, they may get pressed into sand or rocks. Their shells harden, creating the fossil.

Another form of fossil is footprints or tail prints. An animal such as a dinosaur might have left a deep footprint or dragged its tail through the mud. Before that foot or tail print could be wiped away by wind or water, it was covered by sediment and dirt. Then it dried and hardened and was covered by more sediment and pressed into rock, preserving it into a fossil.

Coprolite is another form of fossil. Coprolite is the name of fossilized animal droppings. The animal's waste dried in the sun or extreme cold and then hardened, forming a fossil.

A dragonfly imprint, *above*, and a dinosaur footprint, *below*, were preserved in rocks, making fossils. Fossils are pressed into the ground, and after thousands of years, some of their organic matter becomes fossil fuels such as coal, natural gas, and oil.

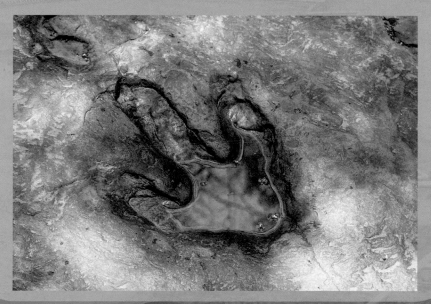

organisms. The gas in your car is from organisms that died millions of years ago! If we continue to use fossil fuels at our current rate, Earth's supplies will run out before more are made.

Another problem you have probably heard about is greenhouse gases. These gases trap more heat into the Earth's atmosphere. They include carbon dioxide, methane, nitrous oxide, water vapor, and ozone. When fossil fuels are burned, they also release extra nitrogen and ammonia into the atmosphere. This can lead to smog, pollution, acid rain, and algae blooms. They can also smother the oxygen humans and other organisms need to breathe, creating toxic environments. All of this contributes to climate change.

It also takes a lot of energy to survey, drill, mine, and transport fossil fuels. They need to be moved by truck or train, which contributes to increasing their **carbon footprint**. A carbon footprint is the amount of carbon dioxide and other carbon compounds that is released into the atmosphere when using fossil fuels. Since trucks and trains require gas, oil, or coal as fuel, they use fossil fuels while transporting other fossil fuels and leave a larger carbon footprint.

Geothermal Energy and Greenhouse Gases

According to the Department of Energy, the carbon footprint of geothermal energy is significantly less than oil, natural gas, and coal. In the table on the right, you can see that geothermal energy sources release less carbon dioxide than fossil fuels. This measure represents how much carbon dioxide goes out into the air when using energy to do things like power lights, computers, TVs, dishwashers, and other appliances that are plugged in. It takes less energy to use geothermal, which means it releases fewer emissions into the air. Geothermal energy has a lower carbon footprint in its delivery systems, too. It does not travel by fossil fuel–burning vehicles. Instead, geothermal energy is moved or transferred from the ground directly into power plants and homes through pipes.

How Many Grams of Carbon Dioxide Are Released Per Kilowatt-Hour of Energy

Energy Source	Grams of CO_2 per kWh
Coal	970
Oil	710
Natural Gas	470
Geothermal	82
Nuclear	66–150
Solar	23–40
Wind	12–20

Pollution

By replacing oil, gas, and coal systems with geothermal energy sources, the world can reduce how much fossil fuels are used and create less pollution. According to the Geothermal Heat Pump Consortium, the amount of geothermal systems currently installed in the United States saves 14 million barrels of crude oil a year (588 million gallons, or 2.2 billion liters). Geothermal systems also use less energy. Depending on the system, they consume 20 to 25 percent less energy than traditional oil and natural gas systems running in a home or building.

When using gas and oil for heat, combustion needs to occur. Combustion is when two molecules come into contact and react with each other, creating heat and light. This is what happens when fire is created.

Geothermal does not need combustion. Nothing new is created; the heat from the Earth is transferred, so it has low or no emissions of carbon dioxide, a major contributor to greenhouse gases. If you get near a geothermal power plant, you will see something that looks like smoke coming from towers outside. It is not pollution, but water vapor. In areas where there is high geothermal energy and geothermal reservoirs, like The Geysers in California and Larderello in Italy, water vapor actually comes out of the ground naturally.

Geothermal power is also considered safer because it does not need combustion to create heat. There is no risk of fire or of combustible gases being released into a building or home. In many homes and buildings, there are carbon monoxide detectors along with fire detectors. Carbon monoxide, or CO, is a gas that is odorless, colorless, and deadly if people breathe it. When gas, oil, and coal are not completely burned, they can give off CO. With geothermal power, there is no risk of carbon monoxide being released.

A Cool Heat

In Chapter 1, you learned about how geothermal systems use heat pumps to transfer heat from the ground into a home. Heat pumps tend to run longer than traditional systems and pump out what is called a **cool heat**. They stay on longer and the heat feels like cooler air than you feel with other kinds of systems. With oil, gas, and coal systems, the area either quickly heats up or quickly cools down to the temperature set on a thermostat and then stops. When the temperature gets a couple degrees off its set temperature, the system starts back up. It is common for people in a home or building that uses heat pumps to ask, "Why is it always running?" Geothermal heat pumps run at a lower, steadier temperature. It takes less energy to run at a steady pace than to turn on and off because of more drastic temperature changes. Some also question the low temperatures. HVAC installers and techs often

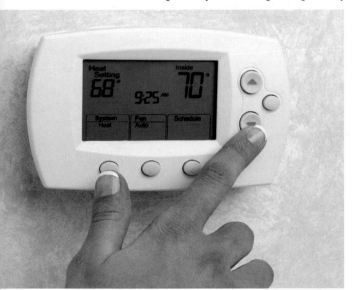

Geothermal heat pumps run at steady, cooler temperatures than oil and gas systems. This takes less energy and means less fluctuation in the temperature of your home.

describe geothermal as a "cool heat." It's a new experience for a lot of customers, but maintaining a more steady heat with a heat pump means less energy and lower costs. The geothermal heating systems are set up to adjust their heat output to match the home or building's actual needs. This is much like new washing machines, which sense how large a load of laundry is and only add the amount of water needed.

Installation and Costs

Another advantage of geothermal is that it can be installed in any building or home, old or new. Gas requires a gas line. Oil requires a tank with regular fill-ups. Coal systems require steady inputs of coal linked to a boiler. If a home or building was not originally built with a gas tank or gas line, installing one requires permission and set requirements from the local municipality. Then the gas company needs to install a line from the gas tank to the home. Or, in some cases, a gas line already exists at the street and the gas company needs to dig from the street to the home to install a line for the gas to run through. With geothermal, it used to be that large areas of a yard were dug up to install an underground system. Modern geothermal systems only require an 8-inch (20-centimeter) hole outside the home to bury the equipment that pulls heat from the ground. That's a smaller area than you need to plant some trees and shrubs!

Geothermal systems have lower operating expenses because they draw energy from the Earth instead of creating new energy the way oil, gas, and coal systems do. They can be used for both heat and air conditioning. Geothermal systems take up less space than large oil tanks that need to be refilled throughout the year. They also do not need

Older geothermal systems required heavy equipment such as this to dig a large hole near a home or business to put the system underground. A newer geothermal system only needs an 8-inch (20 cm) square space for its equipment.

A DEEPER DIVE

Other Renewable Resources

Solar and wind energy are popular alternative sources of energy to fossil fuels. Both are considered clean and do not generate pollution while capturing energy from the wind and sun. They do not give off carbon dioxide or other greenhouse gases. Both can be **cost-effective** over time. The initial setup cost is more than systems using oil and natural gas, but the wind and sun are free sources of energy harnessed by wind farms and solar panels.

There are downsides to solar energy and wind energy, too. Solar energy is only available during the day. That means you have to bank enough energy into a battery on sunny days to carry through sunless days and nights. Pollution can also affect how well the solar panels work. Many homes need more than one panel to generate enough energy, which can be costly. Backup batteries can store energy to be used when the sun is not out, but they can be expensive. However, if you store more energy than your home needs, that energy can be sold back to the electric company, which could cover the costs associated with batteries and panels.

Wind energy is another alternative to fossil fuels, but it's only captured in areas where wind is abundant. In the United States, wind energy is generated in the mostly flat Midwest. Wind energy is a strong force. If we can harness it, it has the potential to provide significantly more power than the whole world needs, but it takes a lot of energy and transmission cables to send wind energy to other parts of the country. Wind turbines can also be noisy and, to some, are not aesthetically pleasing, which makes them a challenge for a home. They are better served grouped together in a field of turbines, which creates energy that is then transferred. Unfortunately, wind turbines are also a threat to birds and other wildlife.

a chimney to vent, like coal. Instead, they use plastic PVC pipes from the geothermal system outside.

It is similar for geothermal power plants or buildings that use geothermal systems instead of fossil fuels. The initial cost is more, but the building or plant will use less energy over time, which will cost less.

The price of natural gas, oil, and coal are always changing. Often, the price changes are blamed on what is going on in other countries that produce oil. But since geothermal energy can be taken right from the ground beneath our feet, the price does not change.

How the Government Helps

When looking to build a new power plant or install a new home heating and cooling system, many only see a geothermal system as costing much more than an oil or gas system. Over time, however, it will pay for itself because it costs less to run day-to-day than other systems.

The government is making it easier to pay for the installation of geothermal systems. Each state has its own program. In general, they include grants and loans for wind, solar, and geothermal energy technologies. It's not just for homeowners but for businesses, economic development organizations, schools, and local governments. That means people can get money from the government to help pay for installing these renewable energy systems.

CRITICAL THINKING

- Explain how fossils make fossil fuels.

- Describe ways geothermal energy has advantages over fossil fuels.

- What are some advantages and disadvantages of other renewable energy sources such as solar power or wind energy?

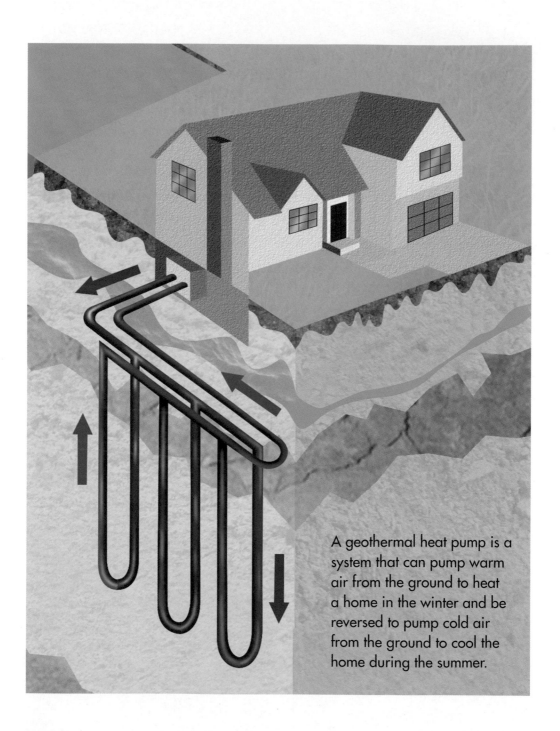

A geothermal heat pump is a system that can pump warm air from the ground to heat a home in the winter and be reversed to pump cold air from the ground to cool the home during the summer.

Chapter 3

The Disadvantages of Geothermal Energy

In Chapter 1, you learned how geothermal energy works by transferring heat from the Earth to heat and cool homes and buildings. In Chapter 2, you learned that geothermal is renewable, clean, efficient, safe, and a viable alternative to replace non-renewable, polluting fossil fuels.

With all these advantages, why doesn't everyone use geothermal energy? There are some disadvantages. Geothermal energy has limitations and creates some pollution. Most of the advantages of using geothermal energy over the long term outweigh the disadvantages. For many, however, the disadvantages are enough to make a different energy choice.

Best for Certain Areas

Geothermal power plants work best in areas where geothermal power is abundant and already bursting through the Earth's crust, such as in California, Iceland, and Italy. As you learned in Chapter 1, these areas are usually along fault lines. In these areas with high volcanic activity, it is easy to harness the energy. The challenge, however, is getting that energy to nearby homes and buildings. Unlike coal, which can be packed

Eyjafjallajökull in Iceland is a volcano covered by an ice cap. The mountain still erupts and remains active, contributing to Iceland's geothermal energy.

onto a truck or train, or oil and natural gas, which can travel by tanker truck, geothermal energy needs a system of pipes to get from the ground to a plant or building. This means companies have to spend a lot of money on digging wells, installing cement casings for **geothermal water** to flow through, and pipes to transfer it to the power plant.

Another disadvantage of geothermal energy reservoirs being located on fault lines is that they are often also tourist areas. People flock to see steam shooting up from the ground. Larderello, Italy, is in the heart of Tuscany. It has a museum so tourists can take a break from the beautiful Tuscan scenery to see how an ancient source of energy steams up through the ground and is turned into modern electricity.

The Strokkur geyser in Iceland throws water into the air every few minutes.

Environmental Impacts

Geothermal plants can cause the land around them to sink. When water and heat are pulled from the geothermal reservoirs, sometimes the rock in the Earth can break and fracture. This causes the ground to shift and sink. One plant in New Zealand is a dramatic example. The ground below it is sinking at a rate of 1.6 feet (0.5 m) per year! This can lead to larger sinkholes in nearby roads and can damage underground pipelines and drainage systems.

The sinking is only considered an issue for geothermal power plants. It is not an issue for homeowners where the geothermal system is small and simply transferring heat from the ground instead of fracturing rock.

Scientists in Iceland consider natural mud pools and other natural geological formations before digging and drilling for geothermal energy. Before building a geothermal power

In Iceland, the muddy ground bubbles and cracks when water and heat are pulled from the Earth to fuel power plants. This can cause the ground to sink.

plant, it is important to consider the trees and wildlife currently living nearby. Will they be moved to another place? How noisy will the power plant be? Will that affect people and animals that live nearby? If the plant is planned for a tourist area, how will it look? What impact does that have on the area and on tourism?

Geothermal Energy and Greenhouse Gases

Geothermal plants are considered much cleaner than fossil fuels. However, they still release trace amounts of greenhouse gases, especially carbon dioxide and hydrogen sulfide. It is natural that water from geothermal reservoirs contains some elements that are toxic to people. These include arsenic, mercury, and selenium. It is important that geothermal energy companies properly protect and insulate the pipes in their systems so that these substances do not make their way into water sources such as wells and reservoirs.

Iceland's government takes precautions to protect areas like downtown Reykjavik from the pollution caused by geothermal plants. Reykjavik is considered one of the cleanest cities in the world.

If wastewater from geothermal plants is disposed of in the right ways, it can mean good things for the

A DEEPER DIVE

Natural Gas Fracking versus Enhanced Geothermal Systems

You may have heard about hydraulic fracturing, or **fracking**. Fracking is a process where sand, water, and chemicals are injected into shale rock at very high pressure to release natural gas. It's a controversial process. Fracking enables us to gather natural gas trapped in rocks. However, it's also blamed for earthquakes, sinkholes, contaminated groundwater, and adding carcinogenic chemicals into the ground while emitting greenhouse gases.

A new process called **Enhanced Geothermal Systems**, or EGS, has been praised by renewable energy advocates as a way to access geothermal energy in more places, but some say it is just as harmful to the environment as fracking. In EGS, fluid is injected into a well to open it with the goal of finding a new geothermal reservoir or stimulating one that has dried up. It was an early test of EGS that caused an earthquake and millions of euros of damage in Basel, Switzerland. The project ended earlier than planned due to fear of more damage and earthquakes.

Since then, the US Department of Energy says it's working on safer ways to use Enhanced Geothermal

Systems. At a project in Newberry, Oregon, twenty seismometers were placed 1,000 feet (305 m) belowground to constantly measure for earthquakes. The seismometers send information about the sounds of the ground fracturing to a computer. This can give indications of how the EGS is affecting the area.

Advocates for EGS say that fracking for gas is done in impermeable rocks. This means it needs significantly more pressure and chemicals to fracture the rocks and keep those fractures open. Geothermal fracking is done in permeable rocks, which means less pressure and only water is needed to generate the heat and energy from the rocks.

Both EGS and fracking have had issues with well blowouts, where pipes containing fracking fluid burst from too much pressure, leaking the fluid into groundwater, nearby waterways, and sometimes drinking water systems. These blowouts have injured workers and caused millions of dollars in damage and cleanup costs. Since EGS uses mostly water and salt water to frack, the risk of pollution and contamination are significantly less than gas fracking.

environment. Reykjavik, Iceland, which heats 95 percent of its buildings using geothermal energy, is considered one of the cleanest cities in the world.

The Environmental Protection Agency (EPA) says that the emissions from geothermal are negligible because they are not combustible. The amount of gases released by geothermal processes are less than those released by fossil fuels. If geothermal replaced gas, oil, and coal, there would still be some release of greenhouse gases but it would be significantly less.

Waste Products

Geothermal power plants do produce a waste product called brine. It is water that has been pulled up from the ground, sometimes with the help of chemicals, and run through a geothermal system, and it contains some harmful metals and minerals. These include corrosive salts, silica, gold, silver, platinum, and hydrogen sulfide. Some plants remove the valuable minerals or recycle them. However, some solid waste from geothermal plants ends up in landfills, which contribute to the creation of methane, a greenhouse gas.

Is Geothermal Energy Totally Renewable?

Geothermal power plants can actually cool the rocks they are trying to harvest hot water and energy from. When companies push cold water into wells to bring the hot water up, it can make the underground temporarily cooler. It is like adding an ice cube to hot chocolate. The hot chocolate is so hot it needs an ice cube before someone can drink it. The ice will quickly melt, but not without cooling the drink a bit first. If the rocks are cooled too much, they might not be able to make enough steam to turn a generator. This would make a geothermal power plant useless.

Geothermal energy production creates small amounts of solid waste. Some of that waste ends up in landfills, which can create more pollution.

By the 1990s, steam pressure at the plant in Larderello, Italy, had dropped by more than 25 percent since the 1950s. The plant was using up steam heat faster than the ground could generate it. The solutions were to dig deeper and dig farther out into nearby areas. Scientists found a much deeper reservoir than they thought existed below Larderello.

At The Geysers in the 1980s, production started slowing down. The plant had thirty wells all pulling steam from the same geothermal reservoir. They were using up the steam faster than the Earth was replenishing it. This is the same thing that happens with coal, oil, and gas. Could Earth run out of steam some day?

One way to solve this problem is to add water. California came up with a plan that solved two problems at once. Local towns needed to find a way to get rid of wastewater and The Geysers needed water. So, treated wastewater was pumped through a 40-mile-long (48-kilometer-long) pipe from Sonoma County and Santa Rosa to The Geysers steam fields.

Adding water is not always the safest solution. It can cause micro-earthquakes. Most are very minor and do not even register on the Richter scale as having magnitude, but, occasionally, the quakes can be more serious. A plant in Basel, Switzerland, was forced to shut down when an earthquake caused damage. There is growing concern regarding Enhanced Geothermal Systems and earthquakes. Any time the rocks underground are being fractured and split, there is a risk they will splinter. If the movement is great enough, small earthquakes can occur.

Dry Rocks Need Water to Make Steam

The Geysers geothermal fields produce dry steam. It's actually hard to find wet rocks underground. The Earth is full of hot rocks, so they need water to produce steam and hot water. In the 1970s, energy companies tried a two-well system. They drilled one pump to send water down and another to pump the hot water up. It was very similar to EGS but was done before companies were able to solve some of the problems. The water fractured the granite, but Mother Nature was in charge. The granite did not fracture the way the companies had planned. Instead, the water they pumped down opened up old fractures in the granite. The geothermal heat and water

Damage caused by earthquakes near geothermal power plants often forces their closure and harms nearby properties and roadways.

went through those fractures instead of coming straight up the pump they had planned for it. The heat and hot water could not be harnessed. The project cost too much. It took two years and a lot of research before the companies were able to try again.

More Upfront Costs

The initial costs of installing a geothermal system are more than fossil fuel–based systems. This is for both power plants and home heating and cooling systems. For geothermal power plants, wells can cost $1 million to $4 million each to drill! Before plants are started, scientists and geologists need to survey the land. Then, they do research about what is below the ground to be sure they are digging wells in the best places to tap the geothermal energy. Since there are not as many geothermal power plants as there are fossil fuel–run plants, this makes it a risky investment. That means people and companies are not as confident using money to pay for all the surveying, researching, and digging needed to find geothermal reservoirs underground. Without the same amount of money being spent on geothermal projects as there are for fossil fuels, it is hard for it to compete. However, the cost of running a geothermal plant is much less than fossil fuel plants.

Drilling for hot rocks is technically challenging. It is not as well known as drilling for oil and gas. There are some risks when looking for geothermal pockets in sandy areas or in shale where wells can collapse. Drilling into granite and bedrock to find geothermal energy can also be very expensive. Geothermal systems can be put anywhere, but the cost of drilling is lower if it is done in an area where there is obvious high volcanic activity.

At home, putting in a geothermal heat pump system can cost around $30,000. That is three to four times more than oil and natural gas systems. But when a home has a geothermal energy pump, its energy bills can shrink by 30 to 40 percent. Most companies say customers will save so much that the heat pump system will pay for itself within five to ten years.

Another disadvantage of geothermal home systems is digging up the yard. As you learned in the last chapter, the holes are shrinking. It used to be that an entire front yard was needed for all the pipes involved in a geothermal home system. Even though the area needed is smaller, some people do not like the idea of having to dig up their yard. Or in some yards, it can be hard to get to the area where the underground pipes need to go. This could mean major re-landscaping if trucks need to go through the yard.

Since geothermal projects are not as widespread as other forms of energy, there are not as many people who know how to install the systems into homes. More people will need training to properly dig in yards to install the pipes for a home geothermal system and to install the heat exchanger inside. Many home geothermal systems use antifreeze and refrigerant. It is important that installers are trained to handle those chemicals.

Geothermal Systems Need Electricity and Maintenance

Geothermal systems need electricity to run. This can be a problem in homes if the power goes out. It means no heat or air conditioning. Homeowners need a backup system such as a generator. Geothermal systems also need regular maintenance. Sometimes systems can frost. This does not just happen when it is cold outside, it can also happen when the air conditioning is running. A service person needs to come defrost it and professionally put it into a defrost cycle.

If the system freezes, the coils cannot produce heat or cold. The frost has to be removed to make it work. If it is cold out and you need heat, heat will not be produced during the defrost cycle. All the heat goes to the defrosting, which can make a home cold. It is helpful to have another heat source such as a fireplace or portable space heaters.

The life cycle for geothermal home systems is shorter in colder areas. It takes more heat to keep homes warm in colder areas. This means the system has to work harder and for longer. Annual service is helpful to keep the system lasting longer.

Slow, Cool Heat

As you learned in the last chapter, one of the things that makes geothermal systems more efficient than other types is that they run slower and at a lower temperature. This can mean more energy and cost savings, but for some, it can mean more discomfort. When the heat is running from a geothermal system, it can actually feel cool coming out of vents. Many are used to instant heat coming from radiators, which are more like hair dryers. As soon as you put on a hair dryer, hot air blows out. You don't have to wait for the air to heat up. Geothermal systems do not work like a hair dryer. The air comes out cool and starts to heat up. It takes time for customers to adjust to the "cool heat" system.

CRITICAL THINKING

- Compare and contrast fracking and Enhanced Geothermal Systems.

- Explain why even though geothermal systems emit some greenhouse gases and produce some waste, they are still better for the environment than fossil fuels.

- Explain how geothermal systems impact the environment.

- Do you think a geothermal heating system would be right for your home? Why or why not?

The US Department of Energy, whose headquarters is shown here, is working to make it easier for companies and families to produce and use more renewable sources of power such as solar, wind, and geothermal energy.

Chapter 4

The Future of Geothermal Energy

The future is bright for geothermal energy. Many people believe its advantages outweigh its disadvantages. However, there are some challenges to geothermal energy use becoming more mainstream.

The US Department of Energy is committed to helping companies make renewable sources of energy like geothermal, solar, wind, and hydrothermal energies easier for customers to buy and use. For instance, they started the Geothermal Technologies Office. The office says it is "vital" that the United States works on developing more geothermal technology because it supplies renewable energy with little greenhouse gas emission. It has two main goals:

1. Accelerate growth. This means making it cheaper to explore areas where there might be pockets of easy-to-access geothermal energy around the country and lowering energy costs.
2. Encourage more companies and homeowners to use Enhanced Geothermal Systems.

MIT Study

The Massachusetts Institute of Technology (MIT) conducted a study on how to better use geothermal energy in the United States. The study focused on Enhanced Geothermal Systems and came up with some ideas. Geothermal energy needs to be more available, sustainable, secure, and cost-effective. It also suggested that if the United States wants to be energy independent and not rely on other countries for oil and gas, the government needs to give geothermal companies at least as much money as oil and gas companies receive. The MIT study stated that the government needed to do more to show that geothermal energy is an important alternative to fossil fuels.

The study showed that companies think geothermal energy looks too risky and this keeps them from building and investing in geothermal projects. Right now, it does cost quite a bit to install geothermal systems. However, if more companies invest in it, costs will go down.

Finally, the study also showed that when it comes to geothermal heat pump systems in homes, there is not a real need for improvements. The systems work really well, but more people need to know about their performance and benefits. Geothermal systems will become less expensive as more homeowners choose them over fossil fuel systems.

Digging Deeper

Another part of the MIT study focused on how to dig deeper and find even hotter resources than are used now. Experts say that there could be two thousand times more energy buried below Earth's surface than we need to

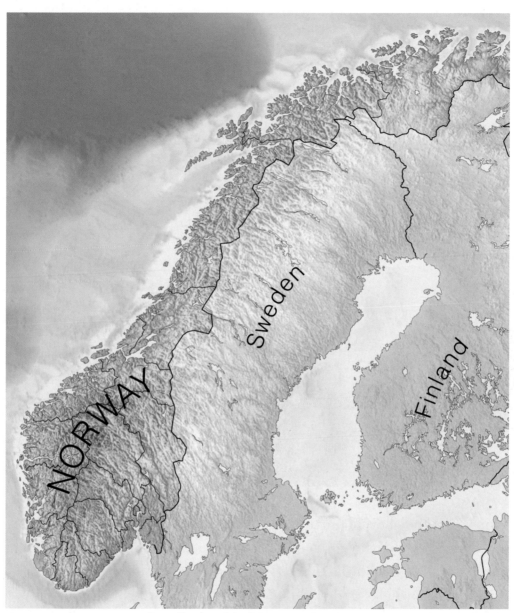

Norway is pioneering the effort to dig deeper wells to hotter areas of the Earth's core. The country is also setting an example of conservation by allowing wells time to reheat and refuel once the groundwater starts to cool the well.

A geyser blows steam and hot water in Norway.

power the United States. Imagine if we could harness that energy!

This is an area where more research is needed. Right now, energy producers are limited in how far down they can dig because the areas get so hot that drills, plastic pipes, and electronics melt, and steel pipes get brittle. Norway is leading the way. Geothermal energy experts there say it may take some time before they develop the methods needed to dig deeper, but they have done it before. Back in the 1960s, Norway took a big, expensive chance and decided to drill into the North Sea to see if there was oil. They hit the jackpot—lots of oil was found. The country is using that knowledge and experience to develop the right equipment to use Enhanced Geothermal Systems (EGS) deeper in the ground there.

Norway is concerned about wells getting cooler over time. They have found that when using EGS, they pump cold water down into the hot ground to pull up the heat. All that cool water can start to cool the ground over time. The plan is to let wells sit for twenty years once they start to cool. That should give them enough time to heat back up to temperatures that are needed to use large amounts of geothermal energy. This makes some people question if using geothermal energy in this way is renewable. Twenty years is a long time to refuel!

Better Drilling

MIT's study suggests that better drilling technology would help geothermal energy become more widely used. The study says EGS is advancing and now we can get into geothermal reservoirs we could not before. EGS can send water into larger rocks than it could before, which allows a drill to get into the rocks and harness the geothermal energy.

There are concerns about how injecting water at such high pressure will affect the areas around the rocks and cause earthquakes. However, drills themselves are improving. We now have better drill bits that can last longer and break through harder rocks. After drilling, casings or pipes have to be placed in the ground to pull the hot water up to the surface. We now have better techniques for making cases that last longer and can endure more water pressure. There are also more durable electronics that can go underground and not melt.

All of these new technologies are making it easier to access geothermal water and energy underground. They are also making it less expensive.

A DEEPER DIVE

Hybrid Power

Hybrid energy projects combine two renewable energies together. When combining geothermal power with solar, wind, or hydropower, it can be more reliable and provide steady streams of energy.

Hybrid projects can be expensive to start up. On the positive side, adding two together can reduce the risks associated with either one. For example, adding solar panels to a geothermal power plant can increase power by adding the solar energy during hot periods of the day. The geothermal part of the plant can supplement when the sun is not out. It also means that companies do not have to dig deeper or newer wells because the solar panels create any extra energy needed. There has been new research in solar-thermal that is creating new technology to make these hybrid projects create more energy and cost less.

Hybrid projects are mostly used for power plants. They can also be used in the district heating systems you learned about in Chapter 1, creating "off-the-grid" power. This means that a building or a home would not need to buy

Pairing solar panels with geothermal energy or wind power is an example of a hybrid energy plan that creates a more reliable and stable source of energy for properties.

energy from an energy company. The building could supply all the energy it needs with solar panels on the roof, a geothermal system in the ground, and batteries to store extra energy.

Ultimately, hybrid energy projects create more stable power at a lower cost while being friendly to the environment. This makes it the kind of project the government, businesses, and consumers want to pay for.

Around the world, countries are looking to develop new sources of geothermal energy. This drill is working on a geothermal energy expansion in New Zealand.

Developing More Sites

The United States and other nations are looking to develop more geothermal power plants. Currently, plants are located near fault lines or in other areas with high volcanic activity. The MIT study pointed out that geothermal energy is always available underground; it's just a matter of pulling the heat up using technology like EGS. It takes more time and money to explore and drill for geothermal energy in areas outside of those with high volcanic activity, but many say that in the long term geothermal is a less expensive energy source and less harmful to the Earth.

Geothermal energy exploration is growing around the world. Africa, South America, Central America, and the South Pacific are all developing geothermal energy plants. In Scotland, the government is funding five new geothermal energy projects.

The United States has partnered with other countries to develop geothermal energy resources. In 2012, the US-East Africa Geothermal Partnership began. The project focuses on Ethiopia, Kenya, Djibouti, Rwanda, Tanzania, and Uganda. It is part of President Obama's Power Africa Initiative, which plans to use US resources and companies to help more people in sub-Saharan Africa get power. The United States is more concerned about using fewer fossil fuels and emitting fewer greenhouse gases because the country uses so much power, but in many parts of Africa, there is simply no power other than generators. Geothermal energy plants and in-home systems could provide much-needed heat, cooling, and electricity in these regions. The project focuses on finding the best geothermal reservoirs underground and figuring out how and where to drill; how to design power plants; how to regulate geothermal energy; how to pay for all the digging, drilling, and power plant building; and how to get equipment to the areas that need it.

More Non-Electric Uses

When geothermal energy is used in a heat pump in a home, it does not make electricity. It simply transfers the heat or cold from the ground to the home. In power plants, however, geothermal energy is primarily used to generate electricity by steam-powering turbines. The MIT study suggests using geothermal water for more non-electric uses. Geothermal water is the hot water that is pumped up from the ground. Instead of using it as energy or to create electricity, the hot water is used directly.

Some places are already setting an example. Growers are using geothermal water to warm greenhouses when outside temperatures are cold. The hot water runs through pipes around the greenhouse and below it to keep it warm. It is used in fish farms to keep the water warm and at the perfect temperature for growing fish. In Klamath Falls, Oregon, geothermal water is piped under the streets and sidewalks. This keeps them from icing and freezing during winter. In New Mexico, geothermal water is piped under fields to keep crops from freezing.

Another creative prospect is using hybrid energy projects with hydrothermal (water and geothermal energies) and solar-geothermal. Google invested in solar companies that are looking at ways to use geothermal energy in combination with solar energy to produce electricity.

While geothermal energy can be found anywhere underground, it can be a challenge to get equipment to some areas. The US is aiding African efforts to use geothermal energy by getting equipment for digging to remote areas.

A DEEPER DIVE

Sustainable Technology

You probably don't know it, but by searching the Internet or using an iPad or iPhone, you are supporting companies who are invested in renewable energy sources. Both Google and Apple are using the latest technologies in geothermal, solar, and wind energy to power their buildings.

Google donated $10 million to two solar companies that use EGS. It started something called the Google Green Initiative, which is working to have a neutral carbon footprint. That means the company will work to reduce its energy use, use more renewable resources, and make up for the greenhouse gases it does emit with other environmentally friendly plans.

Google made changes to its own buildings to reduce its carbon footprint. It uses solar energy and an energy-efficient heating and cooling system that keeps its use to 50 percent less than the rest of the tech industry. Google has also joined with other technology companies to form the Climate Savers Computing Initiative. The group is committed to creating more energy-efficient computers.

Google is even working to reduce greenhouse gas emissions in transportation. It has invested in plug-in cars, offering charging stations at its offices so employees can plug in their cars during the workday. It also offers employees a shuttle service so they can cut down on how many cars employees are driving to work, and employees have started a bike-to-work program.

In 2014, Apple announced it would build a new sapphire plant in Arizona. The sapphires help make iPhone and iPad screens harder. Apple has said it would use renewable energy to power this plant. Apple will use electrical power that comes from geothermal plants in Utah and California.

Apple is committed to using renewable energy sources in other offices, too. The company says its US offices are 100 percent fueled by renewable energy sources with a combination of solar, wind, geothermal, biogas fuel cells, and hydropower. According to Apple, every time you send a text message, FaceTime, or send a photo, the energy Apple uses is renewable and straight from nature.

The Pros and Cons of Geothermal Power

Geothermal energy is used for more than heating homes and buildings. It is also used to warm greenhouses and fish farms, and it can be piped under sidewalks and streets to keep them from freezing in the winter.

Security

What does security have to do with energy sources? Security is important in a few different areas, starting with national security. The United States is involved in wars around the world in areas rich in oil and gas. Some think if the United States could develop more of its own energy resources, it would not be involved in protecting resources in other countries. American troops are sent around the world to places where they are put in danger protecting people and fossil fuel resources.

World events are constantly threatening oil and gas production and delivery to the United States. For example, if two countries begin a war, they could disrupt access to oil. If a US oil company's ship was supposed to pick up oil tankers from one of these countries but cannot get access to the tankers because of the conflict, American homes, vehicles, and businesses cannot use that oil. World events can also affect cost. Oil and gas prices are constantly changing due to conflicts and events around the world.

There are not currently any security issues with geothermal heat. It is in the ground everywhere, not only in specific oil- and gas-rich areas. The MIT study suggests that if the United States starts relying more on geothermal resources along with other renewable energy sources, we would not be subjected to changing prices from other countries or dependent on their security situations.

More Money Is Needed

For geothermal systems to become more widely used, the government and energy companies need to put more money into it. Forty-three states have what are called "renewable portfolio standards." This means that all utility companies have to commit some resources to renewable energy like geothermal, solar, and wind power.

Congress has passed several acts to support giving loans to geothermal energy resources, but many companies do not use them. For geothermal power to thrive in the future, more companies need to take advantage of this money.

As people demand less reliance on fossil fuels, it is more and more important that companies find better ways to produce alternative and renewable energy sources like geothermal energy. Geothermal energy will have to compete against all the renewable sources that will be fighting for their piece of the energy pie. Which will make the most sense and be the most cost-effective to heat and cool homes twenty years from now? Solar? Geothermal? A hybrid? The competition is not limited to the renewables. As geothermal researchers create better drills and methods for drilling wells, natural gas and oil will be able to use those same technologies to make it cheaper for oil companies to get the oil and gas out of the Earth. Geothermal companies need to continue to find ways to make it cheaper and easier for customers.

It will not happen overnight. Studies like the one at MIT and projects in conjunction with the Department of Energy predict it could take until 2030 for geothermal energy to become common in homes and buildings around the United States. They also say it will be worth the wait, as geothermal energy will help better serve and sustain the Earth with its renewable energy.

CRITICAL THINKING

- Explain two things geothermal energy needs to do so more people will use it.

- Explain two ways geothermal energy has already improved.

- Do you think geothermal energy will be a big part of the future of energy? Why or why not?

- Which renewable energy resources do you think will help lower the dependence on fossil fuels in a big way?

Glossary

carbon footprint The amount of carbon dioxide and other carbon compounds that is released into the atmosphere when using fossil fuels.

cool heat The cooler air that comes out when using a geothermal home system. The system runs longer at a steadier temperature.

cost-effective Describing something that produces good results according to how much money is spent.

Earth's core The center of the Earth. It is made up of the inner and outer core. The outer core is liquid. The inner core is a compressed, solid ball of hot metal.

Enhanced Geothermal System A system where water and sometimes other additives are forced into rocks to find geothermal reservoirs.

fossil A preserved trace or piece of an animal or plant. Fossils are the bases of fossil fuels.

fossil fuel Fuel made from fossils that are compressed over millions of years and turned into coal, oil, or natural gas.

fracking A process where water and chemicals are forced into rocks to fracture them and expose natural gas reservoirs.

greenhouse gas These gases trap heat inside the Earth's atmosphere. They include carbon dioxide, methane, nitrous oxide, water vapor, and ozone. They are considered contributors to climate change.

geothermal energy Heat that is generated naturally from the Earth.

geothermal water Water that is naturally heated underground by geothermal energy.

The Geysers One of the first geothermal power plants. It is located in California and started out as a spa where the wealthy took hot mineral baths in the geothermal water. It is now a geothermal power plant.

hybrid energy An energy supply that comes from a combination of different types of renewable energy, such as solar and geothermal.

Larderello The first geothermal power plant, set in Italy. The first public test of geothermal heat to produce electricity was successful at Larderello.

renewable A description of energy sources that can naturally replenish themselves, such as wind power, solar energy, hydropower, and geothermal energy.

solar energy Using the sun's energy to create power and electricity.

wind energy Using the wind's energy to create power and electricity.

Find Out More

Books

Bonnet, Robert L., and Dan Keen. *Gigantic Book of Winning Science Fair Projects*. New York: Main Street, 2005.

Drummond, Allan. *Energy Island: How One Community Harnessed the Wind and Changed Their World*. New York: Frances Foster Books, 2011.

Hansen, Amy S. *Geothermal Energy: Hot Stuff!* Powering Our World. New York: PowerKids Press, 2010.

Krohn, Katherine, Cynthia Martin, and Barbara Schultz. *A Refreshing Look at Renewable Energy with Max Axiom, Super Scientist*. Graphic Science. North Mankato, MN: Capstone Press, 2009.

Snoke Harris, Elizabeth. *Save the Earth Science Experiments: Science Fair Projects for Eco-kids*. New York: Lark Books, 2008.

Find Out More

Websites

Ducksters

www.ducksters.com

Ducksters has resources, information, and learning games for kids. If you type "renewable" into the search box, you will find information on renewable energy and geothermal energy.

Energy Kids

www.eia.gov/kids

This website focuses on information for kids about energy resources. It is managed by the US Energy Information Administration. It has games and activities for students to help learn about using and saving energy along with different types of energy sources.

Kids.gov

www.kids.usa.gov

This is the official portal for kids created by the US government. It has videos, games, and information for kids, teachers, and parents to learn about educational organizations and how government agencies can help kids learn.

National Geographic

www.education.nationalgeographic.com

This is the kids and education part of the National Geographic website. It's full of resources, maps, and videos on energy.

The US Department of Energy

www.energy.gov

This is the official website of the US Department of Energy. Here you can find articles about geothermal energy and other renewable sources of energy, along with information about new technology, maps, and a blog featuring energy facts.

The US Environmental Protection Agency

www.epa.gov

This is the official website of the US Environmental Protection Agency. It is filled with information explaining how Americans use energy and how they can conserve it. It is regularly updated with reports on climate change, water resources, transportation's effect on the environment, and things you can do at home to help the environment.

Index

Page numbers in **boldface** are illustrations. Entries in **boldface** are glossary terms.

Apple, 66–67

Boise, Idaho, 8, 20
brine, 46

carbon footprint, 28–29, **29**, 66
climate change, 28
cool heat, 31–32, **31**, 52
cost-effective, 34, 56, 71

Department of Energy, 9, 20, 28, 44, **54**, 55, 71

earthquakes, 10–11, 14, **14**, 44–45, 48, **49**, 59
Earth's core, 5, 7, **7**, 10, 23–24, **57**
Elliott, William Bell, 8, 19
Energy Policy Act, 9, 20

Enhanced Geothermal System, 44–45, 48, 55–56, 58–59, 63, 66

fossil, 26, **27**
fossil fuel, 5, 13–14, **15**, 23–26, **27**, 28–30, 34–36, 39, 43, 46, 50, 56, 63, 69–70
fracking, 44–45

greenhouse gas, 20, 23, 28, 30, 34, 43–44, 46, 55, 63, 66–67
geothermal energy
  advantages of, 5–6, 23–24, **25**, 28–32, 36, 46, 57, 63, 70
  disadvantages of, 5–6, 39–40, 42–48, **49**, 50–52
  district systems, 8, 16, 20, 60–61
  history of, 4, 8–9, 15–20
  home systems, 11, 16–17, 31–32, **31**, **33**, 36, **38**, 42, 50–52, 56, 64
  how it works, 6–7, 10–11, 16–17, **38**

new developments, 44–45, 55–56, **57**, 58–61, **61**, **62**, 63–64, 66–67

plants, 8–9, 11, 16, 18–19, **19**, **22**, 30, 36, 39–40, 42–43, 46–48, 50, 63–64, **65**, 67

Geothermal Resources Council, 9, 20

geothermal water, 5, **6**, 8, 10, 12, 16–18, 20, 40, **41**, 42–43, **42**, 46, 48, 50, **58**, 59, 64

Geysers, The, 8–9, 19, 30, 47–48

Google, 64, 66–67

Hot Springs, Arkansas, 8, 17

hybrid energy, 60–61, **61**, 64, 71

Iceland, 12–13, **13**, 15–16, **22**, 39, **40**, **41**, 42–43, **42**, **44**, 46

Larderel, Francesco, 8, 19

Larderello, 8, 18–19, **19**, 30, 40 47

Massachusetts Institute of Technology, 56, 59, 63–64

national security, 69–70

Norway, **57**, 58–59, **58**

Old Faithful, 5, **6**

renewable, 5–6, 12, 18, 23–24, 36, 39, 44, **54**, 55, 59–60, 66–67, 70–71

Ring of Fire, 11–12, 14, **14**

sinkholes, 42, 44

solar energy, 23, **29**, 34, 36, **54**, 55, 60–61, **61**, 64, 66–67, 70–71

US-East Africa Geothermal Partnership, 63–64

volcanoes, **4**, 5, 7, 10–12, **13**, 14, **14**, 19, 39, **40**, 50, 63

wind energy, 23, **29**, 34–36, **54**, 55, 60, **61**, 66–67, 70

About the Author

Angela Baker Britcher is an author and journalist. Although her specialty is food writing, she has a strong background in energy conservation, home energy resources, and how to make best use of our personal environments to contribute to making Earth a greener place. She has produced media on energy conservation topics including tips for homeowners and pieces that focus on how those who live in communities along Pennsylvania's section of the Susquehanna River can do more to preserve the watershed's ecosystems and send less pollution to the Chesapeake Bay. She lives in Pennsylvania with her husband, daughter, and springer spaniel. They can usually be found in their yard creating new gardens, working on new ways to make their home more energy efficient, and hiking Pennsylvania and Maryland's state parks.